THE LAUGHING BRIDGE

A Personal History of the Capilano Suspension Bridge

by

Eleanore Dempster

Edited by Marolyn Mahon

Photography by Les Raskewicz

ISBN: 0-9693480-0-2

First Edition June 1988

Published by   *Impressions in Print Enterprises*
                11402 River Wynd
                Maple Ridge, B.C.
                Canada V2X 4Y9
                (604) 467-9140

Printed in Canada by Hemlock Printers Ltd.

Front Cover Photo: Courtesy B. Mahon
                    Capilano Suspension Bridge c.1915

Contents

Preface

The Capilano suspension bridge is a survivor. It was the first business to attract visitors to the Capilano area and is the oldest commercial tourist attraction in the Vancouver vicinity. Built in 1889, the bridge has outlasted other early local establishments — two hotels and at least four tea rooms — on or near Capilano Road.

The Capilano area has been influenced by native Indians, Japanese and Europeans. The suspension bridge embraces all three cultures, from its earliest history to the present.

Three years ago my husband and I took our grandchildren, Paula and Jay, to the canyon as a way of demonstrating part of their history to them. Their great-great paternal grandmother, Mrs. Elizabeth Rebbeck MacEachran, lived at and managed the bridge and its tea house for twenty-five years during the ownership of Edward Mahon, their great-great uncle. While relating this history to them it occured to us that many facets of the bridge story were unknown, and untold.

The idea of writing the history of the Capilano suspension bridge occurred to me on that day in 1985, but it wasn't until 1987 that I considered it as a serious project and started recording oral histories of people directly associated with the bridge. The first contributor was my mother-in-law, Gundrid Dempster, who is the only living former resident of the original cottage built by George Mackay in 1889.

Bryan Mahon was a major contributor, providing me with much information about the era of his father, Edward Mahon. Bryan spent many hours of his childhood at the bridge with his grandmother, Mrs. MacEachran.

This history could not have been written without the input and interest of Rae Mitchell and Nancy Stibbard, most recent owners of the bridge. Their help and support are most appreciated.

Stan Joseph provided information about the native people. His presence at the bridge is a link to its earliest history. Stan's ancestors are the people who called it the laughing bridge.

My deepest gratitude is extended to these contributors for they have made it possible for me to tell Paula and Jay (and now Maryn) the whole story of the Capilano suspension bridge.

Eleanore Dempster
May 1988

Profiles

Gundrid Dempster was born in Vancouver, B.C. April 27, 1895. Her parents were James Knight Rebbeck, mechanical engineer and naval architect, and Elizabeth d'Abbadie Rebbeck. When Gundrid was three years old the Rebbeck family moved to Victoria, where she shared the experiences of growing up with her older sister Lilette and younger brother Waller. Mrs. Dempster entered school at the home of Alice Carr, and later was one of the original boarding students at St. Margaret's School in Victoria.

Mrs. Dempster lived in the original Mackay cottage at Capilano canyon from 1913 to 1915. In 1919 she graduated from Ontario Agricultural College and commenced a career as a dietitian in Ontario. She returned to British Columbia in 1924, where she met and eventually married Robert Dempster of Clayburn, B.C., joining him on the Dempster farm in 1925. Mrs. Dempster lived on the family farm for 58 years, during which time she helped raise three sons and was active in many community organizations. She currently resides in Abbotsford, B.C. and is 93 years old.

Rae Mitchell was born in the Kitsilano area of Vancouver, B.C. in 1910. He attended General Gordon Public School, Vancouver Technical School and the School of Commerce at King Edward High School. Mr. Mitchell's first career was as owner/operator of Mitchell Bros., a plumbing and heating firm which his father and uncle started prior to 1920. He retired from that business in 1951 and purchased the Capilano suspension bridge in April 1953.

Mr. Mitchell has been active in the Greater Vancouver business community as an owner, developer and builder. He lives in West Vancouver, with his wife Evelyn.

Bryan Mahon was born in Vancouver, B.C. June 29, 1913. Until 1928 the Mahon family lived at 323 Burrard Street, which is the site of the present Marine Building. Bryan attended Aberdeen School, King George High School and the University of B.C., studying engineering.

Mr. Mahon was very involved in early aviation in British Columbia. He and two other youthful entrepreneurs operated Columbia Aviation Ltd. at the Vancouver airport, where they offered a flying school, repair shop and bush transportation. Bryan was one of the first employees hired by Boeing of Canada Ltd. when they reopened their Vancouver plant in 1937.

Mr. Mahon moved to Seattle in 1945 and still resides there, with his wife Marolyn. They have two children. He retired from Boeing in 1983 after 46 years of service in engineering and flight testing. He is seventy-five years old and flies his own airplane.

Stan Joseph was born in 1950. He is a member of the Squamish Nation and has lived all his life on their reserve at Capilano, where he learned the ancient skills of carving.

Stan started carving when he was twelve years old, under the watchful eye of his grand-uncle, Chief Mathias Joe Capilano. He grew up with the elders of his people, eventually being initiated as a Spirit Dancer. His Indian name, Sequilem, means spirit traveller.

Mr. Joseph attended Capilano College and Camosun College, studying Northwest Coast art. His totem poles and other carvings have been sold throughout the world.

Nancy Rae Stibbard grew up on Capilano Road in North Vancouver, a short distance from the suspension bridge. She attended Capilano Elementary School, Delbrook High School, and in 1968 graduated from the University of B.C. with a masters degree in psychology.

Nancy married John Stibbard in 1965 and they have two

teenaged children. Prior to becoming involved in running Capilano Suspension Bridge Ltd., Mrs. Stibbard was an active volunteer in her community. She enjoys skiing and playing tennis.

Mrs. Stibbard is the present owner of the suspension bridge complex, which includes the bridge, trading post, Canyon House Galleria and Bridge House Restaurant.

Eleanore Dempster was born in Medicine Hat, Alberta, in 1940. She received her early education in Vancouver and Medicine Hat and later attended Douglas College in Surrey, B.C.. She has been employed as a secretary for School District No. 42 in Maple Ridge, B.C. since 1973.

Eleanore is married to Peter Dempster, son of Robert and Gundrid Dempster and nephew of Edward Mahon, an early owner of the Capilano suspension bridge. It was Eleanore's interest in the Dempster genealogy that prompted her to write this history of the bridge.

Acknowledgments

In addition to those persons mentioned in the preface, I would like to thank the following for their help and encouragement:

June Thompson, North Shore Museum &
Archives
Anna Sumpton, Vancouver City Archives
Marolyn Mahon
Les Raskewicz
Pam Dempster
My family and friends who gave me support,

*and especially my husband, Peter,
for being so patient.*

To Gundrid

1

In the Beginning

In the beginning the Indian people were there. They had always been there.

Three brothers who were shaman giants stood on the shore of the ocean one day and looked north across the water to the mountains. Two brothers were good; the third brother was bad. One good brother threw a rock over the ocean to the northwest. When it landed it wedged between two boulders in a creek near where the people lived in winter. That place became sacred and was called Potlatch. Only shamans and spirit dancers would be welcomed there. They would gather strength from the clear water of the creek and courage from the spirit of the powerful rock.

The second good brother threw a second rock across the water into the north. It landed on the seashore, where a clear mountain creek entered the ocean. That place was called Homulcheson and would be the summer home of the people, where they would be blessed with abundant food from the sea and cedar from the forest. The people would grow strong and prosper there.

The third brother was jealous of his two shaman brothers and the good things they had done for the people. He struggled with them in the ocean but could not overcome their power. The struggle ended when he turned to stone under the disapproving gaze of his brothers. That place became Siwash Rock. It would stand alone in the ocean forever.

Soon after, the elders of a tribe of Stalo people living at Musqueam chose for one of their young men a princess from the

Nanoose tribe. According to the Indian way, when the couple's first male child became of age his mother gave him the royal name Ki-ap-a-la-no. Ki-ap-a-la-no spent his early life at Mahly, near Musqueam, where a mighty river ended its long journey to the sea. He was still a young boy in 1808, barely five feet tall, when a man with white skin stepped onto the beach at Mahly. He was the first white-skinned man Ki-ap-a-la-no could remember seeing, although he had heard stories of others. The man's name was Simon Fraser.

Ki-ap-a-la-no grew to be a very tall, strong man. In time he married and took his bride many miles east into the inland wilderness, where they lived and hunted mountain goats to provide food for themselves and wool for their warm capes. After their first child was born they found life very difficult in the mountains and longed to return to the seaside. They made their way through rugged mountains and eventually came to follow a creek that started slowly in a valley filled with giant cedar and fir trees. The creek, with increasing speed, hurried down out of the mountains and roared through a long narrow canyon with steep rock walls until it finally spent its force quietly entering the ocean at Homulcheson. Ki-ap-a-la-no and his family settled there in the early summer and were soon joined by others. Ki-ap-a-la-no became a great Chief. He was respected by all the people.

From Homulcheson the Indians could fish for salmon, dig clams, and gather cedar for their canoes, baskets and clothing. Homulcheson was a good summer home where the people grew strong and prospered. They were content and lived in harmony with nature and each other.

European surveyors, settlers and missionaries started coming to Ki-ap-a-la-no's area. They recorded the creek that flowed through the canyon as Homulcheson Creek; then changed it and the name of Homulcheson village to Capilano, in honor of the great Chief. The gorge became Capilano Canyon.

Ki-ap-a-la-no was thought to be 83 years of age when he died c.1875. His youngest son, Lahwa, succeeded him as Chief at Homulcheson, now Capilano. All of Lahwa's children died

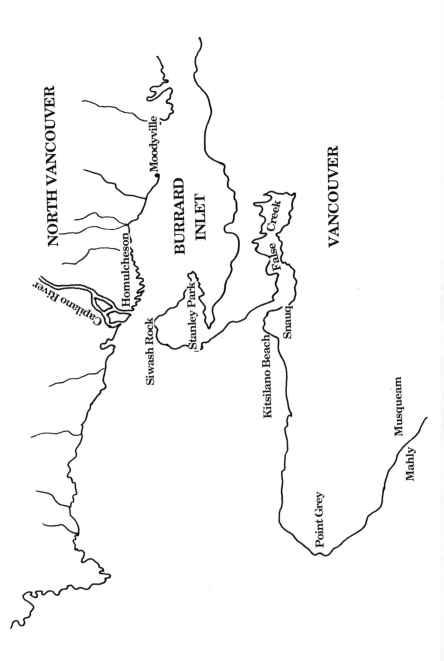

NORTH VANCOUVER

Moodyville

BURRARD INLET

Capilano River

Homulcheson

Stanley Park

Siwash Rock

False Creek

VANCOUVER

Kitsilano Beach

Snauq

Point Grey

Mahly

Musqueam

young and there was no one with direct blood lines to succeed him after his death in 1895. The Squamish people and the church looked to Sahp-luk, or Capilano Joe, as the next leader. He was married to Lay-hu-lette, half grand niece of Chief Ki-ap-a-la-no, and therefore had a link to the royal name Ki-ap-a-la-no. He built a church at Homulcheson and, as his wife was near in blood relation to Chief Ki-ap-a-la-no, he was acceptable to the missionaries and the people as Chief Lahwa's successor. In 1906 the Squamish Indians formally gave Sahp-luk the name Capilano and he became Chief Joe Capilano.

Capilano Joe was a friend of the settlers and helped them in various ways. He was one of two Indian guides who led the Mackay expedition to discover the source of Capilano Creek in 1890. Chief Joe Capilano died March 11, 1910, at the age of 60.

North Shore Museum & Archives   *Chief Joe Capilano*

Lay-hu-lette, also known as Mrs. Mary Capilano, survived her husband and lived on the Capilano Reserve for many years. She was a respected leader of the community and is immortalized in a statue carved by Aage Madsen from a cedar log, which stands in the garden of the Capilano suspension bridge. The carving shows her carrying her son, Chief Mathias Joe Capilano, in a woven cedar basket, called a buh-o-tsoose, on her back. She was believed to be over 100 years old when she died on December 15, 1940.

Chief Mathias Joe Capilano was a carver and spirit dancer.

Stan Joseph: *Chief Mathias started building poles at the bridge in the early '20's. Then he worked there until probably the '40's or '50's. He*

Courtesy N. Stibbard   *Mrs. Mary Capilano*

lived right near the Lions Gate Bridge. Just about under it. He used to carve most of his totem poles there. Big poles. But a lot of them he did actually carve at the bridge. I talked to him a lot before he passed away and he used to tell me about the bridge. August Jack Khahtsahlano was one of the persons who helped them build the first one.

L. Raskewicz   *Totem pole carved by Chief Mathias Joe Capilano*

August Jack Khahtsahlano was born c.1877 at the Squamish village of Snauq, which was where the south end of the Burrard Street bridge is today. He was a great leader, a spirit dancer and storyteller, who was respected by everyone. He has been described as "...a wise man, a courteous gentleman, and a natural historian...a man who could always be trusted".

August Jack was booming logs down the Serpentine River in the days when men were still handlogging. He noted in 1938 that he was retired. He died at Vancouver in June, 1967, when he was about 91 years old.

Vancouver City Archives   *August Jack Khahtsahlano*

August Jack Khahtsahlano once told a friend that in 1889 he and his older brother Willie helped build the first suspension bridge across Capilano Canyon. They dragged two lengths of hemp rope down the side of the canyon then used a team of horses to get them across the Capilano River. They pulled the rope up the other side, anchoring the ends to huge cedar logs that were buried in the ground. More rope formed the support for the shake floor which hung from the main stringers.

Stan Joseph: *The bridge was benefiting everybody. The Indians or whoever was there at the time. It was built from hemp rope, not logging equipment. But all the boards and that were made from old cedar shakes.*

The Indians called it the laughing bridge. When the wind came down the canyon and found the bridge it played with the hemp rope until the bridge started laughing. The wind accepted the bridge that joined the steep canyon walls together and the Great Spirit was pleased.

2

Visions

George Grant Mackay was born at Inverness, Scotland, and lived all but the last five years of his life in the Scottish Highlands near Oban. As a young man he was employed as a civil engineer but later in life became very involved in land development. He was regarded as a man of great ideas and boundless energy who had a futuristic view of his community. At the Glasgow Exhibition of 1883, Mr. Mackay was intrigued by a modest contribution of products and photographs from British Columbia, Canada. He was excited by the suggestion that Vancouver's doors were just beginning to open to the rest of the world. He recognized the potential of the young city and wanted to be a part of its vigorous new growth .

G.G. Mackay wasted no time. In the summer of 1888, when he was 62 years old, he and his family said good-bye to Scotland and made Vancouver their home. He built a large house at 1330 Georgia Street and very quickly became involved in the business community, establishing himself as a reliable and progressive developer with much integrity. One of his first transactions was to purchase District Lots 601 and 607 in the unincorporated District of North Vancouver. In 1888 these lots were granted by the Crown to Edward Vachon and John B. Henderson respectively. Mr. Vachon received his Crown Grant on January 31 and promptly turned it over to Charles Edward Taylor. On September 17, 1888, Mr. Taylor sold District Lot 601 to Mrs. Jessie Simpson Mackay, wife of George Mackay. John Henderson's Crown Grant of District Lot 607 was awarded on October 16, 1888. It appears that a prior arrangement had been made with the Mackays for on October 6, ten days before the signing of the Crown Grant, District Lot 607 ownership was registered to Mrs. Mackay.

By November 1888 the Mackays had successfully acquired 320 acres of timbered land along the east side of the Capilano River (District Lots 601 and 607), from approximately where the present Upper Levels Highway is today, north to just above the first canyon on the Capilano River. George Mackay proceeded to subdivide this acreage and by March 1892, when he, A.P. Horne and R. Mackay Fripp formed the Capilano Park Co., Mackay no

Vancouver City Archives   *George Grant Mackay*

longer owned any of his original 320 acres. He was off and running with greater visions.

Mr. Mackay's dream for the Capilano Valley was unselfish. He desired to develop the 4,626 acres of Capilano Park Co. property north of the first canyon and in the Capilano Valley into a recreational area for the benefit of all citizens. On March 8, 1892, Harry Mackay (George's son) announced plans for an hotel and park in their huge acreage. Neither they nor the government, who sold them the property for $1.00 per acre, recognized the

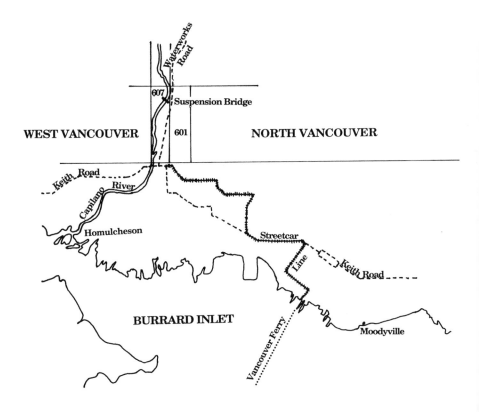

Vancouver City Archives

1330 Georgia Street, between Jervis and Broughton Streets, summer of 1889. Overlooking Burrard Inlet and North Shore mountains.

value of the timber. Or, if they did, they realized the enormous task it would be to get the timber to tidewater. The Capilano Park Co. felt that the real value of the timber was in the enjoyment people would get from being in its midst. It was part of the vision George Mackay had of Vancouver, North Vancouver and surrounding areas.

In 1890 Mr. Mackay anonymously submitted a series of articles to the News—Advertiser, a Vancouver newspaper, in which he made some astonishing prophecies. In them he predicted that in thirty years time a number of leading Vancouver businessmen would make their homes on the north shore of Burrard Inlet. They would travel to their homes from all parts of Vancouver by way of electric streetcars, crossing the First Narrows by a high-level bridge. He even predicted that a huge smelter operated by electricity would process the ores of many mines up the Howe Sound. These predictions were realized with development of the British Properties in West Vancouver and Capilano

Highlands in North Vancouver; the extension of streetcar lines connecting all parts of Vancouver and to a lesser degree North Vancouver; construction of the Lions Gate Bridge in 1938; and discovery of Britannia mines at Brittania Beach on the Squamish Highway.

Unfortunately, plans for the Capilano Park Co. did not materialize. There was a depression in British Columbia in the early 1890's which severely curtailed all development and speculation in the Vancouver area. Land developers such as George Mackay found themselves land poor and if they didn't have substantial capital with which to wait out the storm they became bankrupt in very short order. Mr. Mackay didn't experience much of the depression, however. On January 1, 1893, just five years after arriving in Vancouver full of optimistic dreams, George Grant Mackay died. He had achieved an astounding number of progressive and far-reaching goals between 1888 and 1893 and had laid the foundation for future major economic input in British Columbia. Foreseeing the possibilities of trade with the Orient, Mr. Mackay formed the Oriental Trading Co. which carried on a lucrative business with China, Japan and other Asian countries long before the Canadian Pacific Railway built its first Empress steamship. Together with his sons George and Harry, he operated G.G. Mackay & Sons Real Estate in Vancouver. He was the first man to purchase large tracts of land in the Okanagan and make them available as small farms with a modest profit to himself. He founded the town of Vernon and was known affectionately as the "Father of the Okanagan"; and he was responsible for the first construction on the Capilano suspension bridge site.

When Mr. Mackay visited the Capilano area for the first time he was deeply moved by its wild beauty. In 1888 there were no roads into the area other than a narrow, rough wagon road which ran from North Vancouver a few miles east of the Capilano River to the Vancouver Water Works dam which was under construction at the second canyon. It was called the Water Works Road and later Capilano Road. There were no farms, no houses; nothing but virgin forest and the river.

Soon after acquiring his property, an Indian led him to a precipice at the first canyon from where a spectacular view was seen up and down the river. Mr. Mackay decided that he would build his retreat — his cabin — at that place, to get away from business pressures and enjoy the quiet solitude of the forest when the need arose.

Considering that Mackay acquired the property in October 1888, and that snow started in that region in November, it is reasonable to assume that construction of the cabin didn't start until the spring of 1889. He contracted with two Scottish country-men to build a four-room cottage on the very edge of the canyon, with a verandah at both ends and along the entire west side, which was the canyon side, so one could enjoy the view both ways on the

Courtesy B. Mahon   *Etching of cliff house c.1905*
Note second building at left.

river. It was constructed of rough cedar lumber and shingle siding hewn from trees on the property. The roof was steep enough to carry the weight of heavy snow in winter and finished with thick cedar shingles. It was a primitive but comfortable cottage from which Mr. Mackay, his family and friends, could enjoy the pleasures of natural surroundings. In deference to his love for the area and his Scottish origin, Mr. Mackay soon became known as the "Laird of Capilano".

A short distance north of the cabin, and set back from the cliff's edge, was a second structure which served as a combination bunkhouse and storeroom. Built from the same material as the cabin, this building was contoured to the ground and had several levels, each one determined by the height of the solid rock upon which the framework rested. The buildings were finished by June 1889, and became the first residence in what would later be one of North Vancouver's early prestigious residential areas.

Vancouver City Archives   *Group photo at Mackay's cabin c.1900*

Vancouver City Archives   *Group of adventurers at Mackay's cabin c.1900*

Getting to Mackay's cabin was not easy. In 1889 transportation across Burrard Inlet was via the steamer Senator, a Union Steamship Co. vessel that called occasionally at North Vancouver en route from Moodyville to Vancouver.

Vancouver City Archives   *Passengers aboard the S.S. Senator, about to cross Burrard Inlet, c.1893*

A horse and buggy could be taken on the Senator but the horse had to be taken out of the shafts and the buggy and horse placed crosswise on deck. There was a shelter for about twenty passengers. Visitors to Mackay's would take the Senator to North Vancouver and travel by horse and buggy up the rutted Water Works Road to the cabin. Or, if they had no horse, would walk the six miles there and six miles back, the ladies in long dresses that tugged at the ground with every step; the gentlemen wearing high stiff collars and ties that threatened their every breath; everyone carrying his or her share of the provisions needed to exist for one or two days. One had to be an avid lover of nature to get up very early in the morning, pack enough food for the day, hitch the horse to the buggy, take a slow boat trip across the inlet and ride six miles up a bumpy wagon road to an isolated cabin on the very edge of a 200' canyon with nothing between life and the river below but a rough pole verandah that quivered with every kiss of the breeze. No wonder G.G. Mackay had visions of electric streetcars and high-level bridges!

In 1889 the Vancouver Water Works dam was completed and the water turned on in Vancouver homes on March 25.

Vancouver City Archives   Capilano Dam, 1888

That same year August Jack Khahtsahlano, his brother Willie and others are said to have constructed a hemp rope bridge across the first canyon of the Capilano River at a point about 200' south of Mackay's cabin. One can only speculate on the reason for the bridge. Logging in the area wouldn't start until 1902, and the Vancouver Water Works dam was reached by way of the wagon road on the east side of the river. It may have been useful to Mackay and his friends as an access to the west wall of the canyon, where it was possible to climb down to the river to fish. The east face was too dangerous to descend. Or Mackay may have wanted to cross the river there so he could trek through the magnificent forest west of the canyon. Whatever the reason, the bridge was in place and would play a significant role in attracting visitors to the Capilano area.

3

Into the
20th Century

I t is not known why George Mackay sold his property at the
first canyon. Perhaps he felt it was not a significant parcel in
relation to the Capilano Park Co. proposal; it may have been his
intention from the outset to subdivide the property and open up the
area; or it may simply have been a matter of economics because
of the existing depression that was badgering the population at
that time. Whatever the reason, he subdivided and sold his
holdings in District Lots 601 and 607 to wealthy businessmen,
most of whom resided in Vancouver. The major purchasers were
James Cooper Keith, manager of the first bank in Vancouver, the
Bank of British Columbia; Otto Semisch, land developer and
attorney; and Bruno Stelzer, a wealthy speculator from Breslau,
Germany. Mr. Stelzer purchased Block 25 of Subdivision 3,
approximately 24 acres containing the site of Mackay's cabin, the
bridge and a considerable piece of timbered land on the west side
of the river in November 1892, through his agent Otto Semisch.

Mr. Semisch and his wife were apparently living at the canyon
in 1894, when he was described as ...*a short man with a grey
complexion who drove down to the ferry in a small buggy hauled
by a white horse, his wife with him.*

It is not known if Mr. Stelzer actually visited his land on the
Capilano River, but others did. The Mackay cabin became a very

popular destination for weekend hikers and picnickers in the Capilano area. A particularly avid group of wilderness lovers, who were also Vancouver businessmen, were frequent visitors with their wives and friends. They became known as the "Capilano Tramps" in reference to the long "tramp" up to the cottage from the ferry landing. They are pictured here in May 1896.

Vancouver City Archives   *The Capilano Tramps, May 25, 1896*

Bruno Stelzer held the property for 17 years. During this time one significant improvement was made that would ensure the preservation of the property as a recreational site. Mr. Stelzer authorized construction of a steel cable suspension bridge 450 feet long to span the canyon. Otto Semisch, who has often been referred to as the person responsible for building the first steel cable bridge over Capilano Canyon, had acted as Stelzer's agent over the years, making whatever arrangements were necessary for use of the cabin and other amenities of the site. In 1903 he took charge of arrangements for building the bridge and contracted with William T. Farrell to carry out construction. On April 20, 1903, the Daily Province newspaper reported that

> ... Plans have been prepared by Mr. W.T. Farrell
> for a suspension bridge over the Capilano Can-
> yon, which will span the chasm at a height of 200
> feet. The bridge will be constructed to stand a
> strain of sixty tons, which should be ample for any
> footbridge. At one end of the bridge a stairway will
> be constructed leading to the bottom of the can-
> yon. This will afford access to the natural garden
> down in the canyon, besides being more conven-
> ient for fishermen. It is intended to commence
> work at once, so as to have it available for visitors
> to that locality during the present summer.

Mr. Farrell fulfilled his contract and the bridge was constructed with two single strands of steel cable strung across the
canyon and anchored to huge logs buried in the ground and
mounded over with rocks and earth.

On August 8, 1904, The Daily Province reported that Vancouver and North Vancouver city officials and many invited guests
representing Vancouver's financial elite

> ... inspected the Capilano Dam on Saturday last.
> ... On the way up the Capilano the party stopped
> at the gorge and many took the run across to the
> further bank on the suspension bridge at that
> point.

The reason for construction of this steel cable bridge may have
been simply to provide a less challenging crossing for visitors than
that provided by hemp rope. As suggested in the Daily Province
article, the site was recognized as a popular location for hikers and
fishermen. Mr. Stelzer and Mr. Semisch, being astute businessmen, may have been responding quite naturally to the growing
demand for recreational access to the area.

Construction of the bridge may have been linked to logging
activity which had started on the west side of the river. In 1903 the

"THE NERVOUS BRIDGE"
CAPILANO CANYON
VANCOUVER, B.C.

TIMMS

Vancouver City Archives   *The original steel cable bridge across*
Capilano River at the first canyon, 1904.

CAPILANO CANYON N VANCOUVER BC

Vancouver City Archives

Visitors crossing the Capilano suspension bridge, 1905.

Capilano Lumber Co. established a mill at Sisters Creek and started harvesting the beautiful cedars which were in great demand for shingles. W.T. Farrell was a partner in the Capilano Lumber Co. He was also instrumental in forming a syndicate for construction of a shingle bolt flume to run through the first and second canyons. This flume linked up with one constructed by the Burrard Inlet Flume and Boom Company which came from Sisters Creek to the second canyon, and with the flume owned by Dr. John Thomas Carroll which ran from the lower end of the first canyon 3-1/2 miles along the river to its mouth near the Mission Indian Reserve, where the shingle bolts tumbled into Burrard Inlet and the holding pond. The syndicate that Mr. Farrell formed consisted of himself, Dr. Carroll, and R. Kerr Houlgate. In consideration for building the canyon section of the flume the Capilano Syndicate was to share in the business resulting from the completed flume.

Vancouver City Archives   *Shingle bolt flume, c.1911*

Construction of the flume through the canyons was under way when the North Vancouver Express reported the following on August 25, 1905:

> *The other day W.T. Farrell, superintendent of the sawmill above the Capilano Dam, slid some 80 feet into the canyon and fell about 15 feet onto a rock, sustaining severe injuries. He was engaged at the time on the flume.*

James W. Morton states in his book *Capilano — Story of a River*:

> *...On February 13, 1906, one of the longest flumes in America was completed. It ran from Sisters Creek, almost nine miles from the inlet, down the western bank of the river, past the dam and into the Second Canyon; it was between 100 and 200 feet above the racing water, and clung precariously to the rock face. Capilano Joe's Indians and the Japanese had built it. Some had been killed in the process and were buried high above the water on the plateau of the canyon....*

In April 1906 the Burrard Inlet Flume and Boom Company merged with the Capilano Syndicate and became the Capilano Flume Company. William Farrell was one of the directors and also the manager.

Gundrid Dempster: *Across the bridge was a flume. As children we had walked that flume to second canyon. In the second canyon it was really breathtaking, as the flume skirted laboriously around cliffs, over gullies, with rushing, roaring river many feet below. On passing one saw the famous salmon pool; deep greens, inde-*

scribable loveliness, the river gliding into roaring rapids so that there is a continued presence of that river though one sees it or not.

The flume went all along the western banks from above the second canyon down towards the Keith Road bridge. Shingle bolts were cut by Japanese and floated down the flume to the shingle mill. Yes. It was quite exciting. You never knew whether the flume was going to be full with logs or not. And this was one of the things that was rather a nightmare, because my brother wanted to ride them. It was a great thrill to try to ride on a bolt, or watch the bolts rushing by without a mishap. But sometimes when they were coming down too quickly they would shoot up into the air and go down the 300 feet. Sometimes, too, when they'd get too many they'd shoot up into the air and they'd break the flume and then all the water would go down. The Japanese would have to get busy and mend it and get water going in the flume.

The shakebolts were coming from mills on the west side, by the Japanese. Here and there would be little Japanese settlements, actually. In some of the Japanese camps, amongst their houses, was usually a bath house built of wood. Built in such a way that fire could be built under the wooden tank in which they bathed themselves. Why these strangely constructed buildings did not burn down we children could not fathom!

It is easy to deduce that the suspension bridge, with its cottage and bunkhouse, would be useful to the men logging nearby in 1903 and later working on the flume. It was a tedious 9-mile trek from Burrard Inlet to Sisters Creek where the Capilano Lumber

Capilano Canyon and Flume, Vancouver. B.C.

North Shore Museum & Archives

Co. operated its shingle mill. It would have been very convenient for the men to stay at the cabin and cross to the west bank of the river over the suspension bridge.

Edward Mahon purchased the Capilano Flume Co. from William T. Farrell et al two years before acquiring the bridge property. On May 4, 1908, he wrote to a friend in England —

> *... I have bought the Capilano flume which runs from about a couple of miles north of the Dam down to the First Narrows, together with some timber up the Capilano. I have also bought a little mill and am leasing it to some Japanese, who are going to cut timber on their own property up the Capilano and pay me $2.00 per thousand for the use of the sawmill and the flume....*

Leasing to the Japanese was a significant business transaction in 1908. Japanese and Chinese people were discriminated against by all levels of British Columbia society and measures were instituted by government to prevent them from attaining success

Courtesy B. Mahon

Timber in the Capilano Valley, c.1908.
E. Mahon, two unidentified loggers,
W.T. Farrell

Courtesy B. Mahon

E. Mahon sawmill leased to Japanese 1908.
W.T. Farrell on platform, holding stick;
E. Mahon standing on ground

in the lumber industry and other areas. Mr. Mahon treated the Japanese loggers fairly and earned their respect. They responded to his kindness in an unexpected way.

Bryan Mahon: *Dad mentioned to his employees that he'd like to have a little log cabin up the Capilano, but he didn't supervise them because he was busy with his other affairs. Perhaps out of respect for him they built a house which was much larger than a little cabin. Since they were Japanese they made a roof curled up at the edges in oriental style. It had quite an individual character. It was very much larger than he had in mind. The "log cabin" is now part of the community centre of a housing development called Spuraway on Keith Road.*

At the log cabin they cleared a large area and imported azaleas and rhododendrons from the Orient and made a big nursery. Then, after developing the plants, they replanted them all up and down the boulevards in North Vancouver and some of them are still growing.

Dad finally sold the log cabin to a Mr. Herman. Mr. Herman liked horses, so he made a riding ring and that's how it got the name of Spuraway.

Courtesy B. Mahon   *The log cabin under construction, c.1909*

Courtesy B. Mahon   *Painting of the log cabin, c.1909*

44

In 1909 Bruno Stelzer decided it was time to sell his little piece of Canada. In October that year William Dick purchased the property for $11,000. under agreement for sale to Stelzer. Then between September 1910 and July 1911 an intricate financial package was put together involving Stelzer, Dick, Edward Mahon of Vancouver, his brother Gilbert Mahon of London, England, and James Cooper Keith, also of Vancouver. When the final t's were crossed Edward Mahon had purchased the property with an investment of $375. and J.C. Keith held the agreement for sale valued at $11,000. Mr. Stelzer had relinquished his property to energetic pioneer developers and it was about to take on a new look.

4

Years of Growth

Edward Mahon was born in Rawmarsh, Yorkshire, England in 1862. His ancestral home was Castlegar, Ahascragh, Co. Galway, Ireland, which became the family residence of his eldest brother Sir William Henry Mahon, Baronet. Edward came to British Columbia about 1889 with his younger brother Gilbert. Soon after arrival they became involved with mining in the Slocan and Nelson areas. They established a small camp there and called it Castlegar, after their home in Ireland.

Bryan Mahon: *My grandfather was an Anglican minister with a parish in Rawmarsh, Yorkshire. My father, Edward, got a liberal education at Oxford and he studied to be a minister. However, he lived at a time when scientific knowledge was advancing with the theories of Darwin and others and he felt that the ministry, with its strict literal acceptance of dogma, was not for him. He then studied law and was admitted as a solicitor in the courts of Ireland.*

Both his early starts at a career conflicted with his very strong sense of ethics and integrity, so he decided to be a pioneer in British Columbia, arriving about 1889. He told me with a twinkle in his eye that "you can make money out of real estate and business without telling lies".

Courtesy B. Mahon   *Lilette, Edward and Bryan Mahon, c.1914*

Dad's brother John had come to Vancouver on a ship from England and had concluded that Vancouver was going to be a tremendous metropolis because it was the only British port of consequence in the North Pacific and would be on an important trade route to the Orient. So, therefore, the idea of starting the town of North Vancouver was going to be a major long-term investment.

John continued to live in London and delegated the North Vancouver Land & Improvement Co. management to his younger brother Edward, my father, who was president. That company subdivided North Vancouver from bush, sold lots and laid out the streets.

Edward Mahon and George Mackay circulated in the Vancouver community and very likely knew each other as business acquaintances and, perhaps, friends. George Mackay's dream was for a recreational wonderland in the Capilano Valley; Edward Mahon's vision was of a beautiful, prosperous town on the north shore of Burrard Inlet. Mackay died before he could fulfill his dream; Mahon accomplished his goal by developing the town of North Vancouver and, to some degree, achieved Mackay's objective by establishing the Capilano suspension bridge as a major recreational attraction.

Edward Mahon was a 48-year-old bachelor when he bought the Capilano bridge site in 1910. He had plans for marriage, however, and the bridge played an important role in realizing those plans. Mr. Mahon was in love with Lilette Rebbeck, the young and beautiful daughter of James Knight Rebbeck of Victoria, B.C.. Mr. Rebbeck was a friend of Edward's who had died in May 1910, leaving his wife Elizabeth, two daughters, Lilette and Gundrid, and a son Waller.

Courtesy G. Dempster   *Lilette, Waller, Gundrid Rebbeck, c.1910*

Elizabeth Rebbeck, her daughter Lilette and three Japanese servants, Toby-san, Yui-san and Yanke-san, moved from Victoria to the cottage at Capilano canyon in October 1910. By the end of November the Japanese family had increased by one, as Yui-san gave birth to a baby girl at the canyon. 15-year-old Gundrid and 12-year old Waller remained in boarding school in Victoria.

Courtesy G. Dempster   *Elizabeth Rebbeck, c.1920*

Vancouver, B.C., 13 Oct. 1910
My dear little girl,

We went up to Capilano on Monday. It was a beautiful day and everything looked lovely. The house has to be cleaned and arranged a bit, so that we won't be able to go up till next week, but the Japanese are there already, all three and happy to have got to the end of their journey.

...There is a nice big drawing room at the bungalow and you and Waller will be able to dance all you want when you come. You will love it at the canyon and the nice old bungalow will make a nice home...
Your loving mother, Elizabeth Rebbeck

Lilette also wrote.

Vancouver B.C., 16 Oct. 1910
Dearest Gundrid,

Mother and I are still at the Findlay's. We hoped to go up to Capilano tomorrow for good, but Mr. Gardener, the architect who has charge of the repairing of our house, rang up just now to tell us that the house will not be ready for us till Wednesday. ...

I loved the little house at the Canyon. In time when everything is arranged inside it will be very warm and cosy. It is built on the edge of the Canyon and there are the most beautiful views from the verandah and from the swing bridge which I crossed with Mr. Gardener. ...I am looking forward so to living at the Canyon. ...

Courtesy B. Mahon   *Japanese mother and child at Capilano, c.1911*

Bryan Mahon: *The house that she lived in was right on the edge of the canyon. If you got out on the balcony you would look down 200 feet. It was almost overhanging the precipice. There was another one just up the hill that they called the bunkhouse. It was covered with cedar shakes on the outside, I remember that. I was not encouraged to go to the bunkhouse because if a small child fell over the edge that would be the end.*

Gundrid Dempster: *We lived in the little old house on the cliff north of the teahouse. The cliff house. Looked to have been built as for a weekend or holiday place. A long house. At either end was a big room the full width of the house, with a big fireplace in one end and a big fireplace in the other end. Large windows made most of the end walls. A bathroom and cupboards were added when we came to live in it. One big room we made into the kitchen and the front of the fireplace was covered over. We had to use lamps and candles. We had a stove, too, in the hall. The wood was shingles, all handmade; everything was handmade all the way through. 300 feet down to the river. It was a lovely spot. Mist used to come up. It was really quite fascinating. You could see the water, the river down below. There was a plum tree right beside our house. The most marvelous plum. And an apple tree.*

There was another house beyond the cliff house. We called it the bunkhouse. It was built on the higher cliff, with a view from its big room of the river just as the river makes a turn. This bunkhouse was made of hand-hewn cedar shakes. Each room on a different level as the building followed the unevenness of the rock bluff. A hallway went through the centre with steps when needed. Two rooms on the garden side, a storage room and a place for fuel. Men from the waterworks stayed there sometimes. Up on a higher level again was a small shed which we used for the chickens but may have been used for a cow or horse when the bunkhouse was inhabited. Also made of homemade cedar shakes and timbers.

The plan was for Mrs. Rebbeck to live at and manage the suspension bridge, thereby providing an opportunity for her to generate an income and establish a permanent residence at the same location. Some improvements had to be made in order to encourage more sightseers to visit the canyon and Edward wasted no time in this regard, particularly since the tram line had been recently extended to Capilano Road. Early in 1911 he approached William Farrell with his plan for a teahouse on the grounds and asked him to submit an estimate for its construction.

March 1, 1911
Dear Sir,

I will build your house at the wire bridge Capilano according to plans and specifications submitted to you in a good and proper workman like manner for the sum of two thousand seven hundred and sixty-two dollars.

If we include the painting and plumbing within the rooms upstairs, one of them being a lavatory over the kitchen, then the price would be $3,200.00, the work to be commenced forthwith and rushed to completion.

Yours truly,
W.T. Farrell

Courtesy B. Mahon

Unidentified person, W.T. Farrell, E. Mahon, c.1911

Interior view of tea house, May 1911

An open-air porch overlooking the canyon.

Courtesy G. Dempster   *Exterior view of tea house, 1911*

Vancouver City Archives   *Mrs. Arthur C. Buswell & daughter,*
                                        May 24, 1911

The teahouse was completed in time for the May 24th holiday celebrating the Queen's birthday. The final cost was approximately $4,500., considerably above the original estimate of $3,200. It was situated about 100 feet from the cliff house and set close enough to the edge of the canyon that it became an extension of the canyon wall. From the enclosed verandah overlooking the gorge a visitor could look straight down without restriction to the river rushing over rocks at the bottom of the ravine. It was a little less spectacular than the dropoff from the cottage where the verandah seemed to jut out over the cliff, but none the less thrilling for a sightseer.

Courtesy G. Dempster   *Cliff house, tea house, bridge, c.1911*

Bryan Mahon: *They called it the teahouse. That's the only name I know of. I remember that the kitchen was at the north end and the tea room at the south end. And the tea room was long. The teahouse had two gables that went in an east-west direction. At one end it looked towards the road and at the other end it looked towards the canyon. Then there was another section going between the two gables. The construction — you see, they were planks which went through a machine that rounded the edge like a log. They weren't prefabricated, there was just a pile of these planks. They were rounded in the sawmill and then just piled in a pile and nails were driven down through the planks. There weren't any frames. Just 3x8's in a pile. Very unusual construction, but at the price of lumber you could afford to do it that way.*

After the teahouse was built Mrs. Rebbeck focused on the gardens. The grounds around the cabin and bridge had been cleared previously and an attempt had been made to create an attractive area where visitors could sit on the grass and eat a picnic lunch. Edward and Elizabeth wanted to improve the sparse landscape and develop a garden in which people could stroll at a leisurely pace, enjoying the fresh air and mountain setting. They did this with the help of their Japanese workers. Mrs. Rebbeck was an avid landscape designer and gardener, having had previous experience in French Indochina where she had managed a small business exporting her own seeds to England and France.

Daffodils, crocuses, primulas, roses and a large selection of perennial plants soon brightened the walkways. Rhododendrons and azaleas from Mr. Mahon's nursery were added along with other shrubs, small ornamental trees and fruit trees. A few of those early rhododendrons are still in place on the grounds; large shrubs that have survived summer sun and winter snow over the years to add character and history to the garden. Features of a terraced rock garden that was created behind the bunkhouse also remain.

Courtesy G. Dempster   *Capilano Suspension Bridge Garden, c.1912*

Courtesy B. Mahon   *Entrance garden, Capilano*
                                     suspension bridge, c.1913

Courtesy G. Dempster   *Terraced rock garden, c.1913*
                                  Note corner of bunkhouse at left.

Capilano Road, c.1910

By 1914 the Capilano suspension bridge had become a favorite destination for people desiring a quiet day in woodland surroundings with a touch of civilized gentility. It didn't matter that the trip there was still quite lengthy, even though electric streetcars were now in existence.

Bryan Mahon: *Since most people didn't have cars, they*
                      would take the electric trolley car down to the
                      ferry dock in Vancouver, go across to North

Vancouver on the ferry, then catch the trolley car to Capilano and just ride on that until it got to the end of the tracks, which was at the Capilano Road.

North Shore Museum & Archives

Streetcar terminus at Capilano Road, c.1912

Then they'd walk up the Capilano Road to the suspension bridge. Well, that's a distance of a mile, or a mile and a half, something like that. So, people would be carrying a picnic basket and towing a lot of kids and they'd have a couple of miles by the time they got there and back again; three miles, or four miles of walking. And then they would go through all these trolley cars and ferry boats to get to the place they came from in Vancouver. This was an outing, but it wasn't with the benefit of automobiles. There were taxi drivers who waited at the end of the trolley car. There was Harry

Gooch, who would bring people from the trolley car to the bridge in his taxi, which was a Model T. Ford, or something like that.

North Shore
Museum & Archives
(A.Elliott photo)

The "Golden Staircase" c.1908. These steps were a shortcut over a rock bluff, rejoining Capilano Road near the suspension bridge entrance.

Later on there were tour busses. A popular one was operated by the City Taxi, Auto and Sightseeing Co.. Another was the Terminal City Motor Co. Ltd., which ran open touring cars designed to hold about 30 passengers. These cars were painted green and had 6 bench seats. Tour #3 went to the suspension bridge, Canyon View Hotel and Tipperary Tea Gardens. It left twice a day from the main office across from the Vancouver Hotel on Georgia Street in Vancouver, took 4 hours for the round trip, and cost $2.00 per person.

Motor clubs often included the suspension bridge in their outings, taking pride in shortening their travel time with each visit. On June 23, 1912, Mrs. Rebbeck wrote to her daughter Gundrid:

> *...Tomorrow we are going to be very busy at the teahouse. We are going to give luncheon to 200 people. I hope it will be fine, the roads are in splendid condition after the rain. The Vancouver Motor Club is entertaining the Seattle Club and they are coming up to Capilano, having luncheon here.......*

City of Vancouver Archives   *Early sightseeing car, c.1918*

Gundrid Dempster: *You see, what we were up against was the weather. If you didn't have fine weather you didn't have anybody at the bridge—you didn't have anybody at the teahouse. And that was the nightmare of it. Sometimes there might be three hundred people and sometimes only about fifty. So, the awful part about it was that mother would prepare—like the 24th of May, a big holiday—for a lot of food and then it would rain and nothing happened. So it was a really hectic existence. She made ham sandwiches and ice cream and sometimes they'd have fillets for an outfit that was coming. It had to be special.*

The food angle was very difficult. We didn't have a proper way of keeping things cool. Mother only had a little icebox. Then we also had the difficulty of getting ice for the icebox. You had a tiny little box for three hundred people, if they came, and if they didn't come you had it all going bad. It was no bed of roses, let me tell you.

Bryan Mahon: *My father made me a little toy automobile that you drove with bicycle pedals and I had that up at the canyon. At the bridge they used to sell ice cream cones and so forth. To keep the ice cream cold they needed ice. I would peddle back and forth to where the ice came from and deliver the ice back to the tea room with my bus for a nickel.*

B. Mahon in jitney (taxi) used to transport visitors from streetcar terminus to suspension bridge, c.1924

The Duke and Duchess of Connaught visited Vancouver in 1912. The itinerary of the Duchess and Princess Patricia included an escorted tour to Capilano Dam, with an unscheduled stop at the suspension bridge. They may have been the first royal guests to enjoy the beauty of the first canyon. Mrs. Rebbeck described their visit in a letter to her daughter Gundrid.

Capilano, 22 Sept. 1912

...We had a delightful surprise yesterday afternoon. Her Royal Highness the Duchesse of Connaught and Princess Patricia came up to the bridge. They seemed to enjoy the bridge very much. Afterwards Her Royal Highness expressed herself as willing to look into the Canyon from my house and asked me to show her the way. I took her through our little house and through the drawing room and she said "What a dear little house!", and all sorts of other nice things. Then she talked very nicely to me and I had her for 15 minutes all to myself. Then we went back through the Teahouse and Her Royal Highness thought that it was

Vancouver City Archives

Duke & Duchess of Connaught arriving at CPR station, Vancouver, September 18, 1912. It was the Duke's first visit as Governor-General of Canada.

*all so pretty and nice and thanked me and shook
hands. I did enjoy her so much and everybody was
so surprised because they thought that they were
going to the top of the hill...*

The number of visitors to the bridge increased every year and
in 1914 Mr. Mahon became concerned about the strength of the
cables. He consulted the firm of Cleveland & Cameron, civil and
hydraulic engineers and surveyors, for a professional estimation.

Bryan Mahon: *Dad got an engineer named Cameron to
                 investigate the structural integrity of the
                 bridge and recommend changes that would, if
                 necessary, make it properly safe. Cameron
                 recommended doubling up the suspension
                 cables. The original cables were of a more
                 flexible type similar to cables used in the
                 logging industry; the second set of cables that
                 Cameron recommended putting in were more
                 suitable to suspension bridges — less flexible
                 construction. There were two cables on each
                 side, one with a larger diameter than the other.
                 The larger diameter one was the flexible
                 cable; the smaller one was more like solid steel
                 and was more suitable for a suspension
                 bridge. The cables ran through a big concrete
                 block — oh, I don't know, it might be a
                 20'x20'x20' cube — that's what's holding the
                 bridge up.*

Mr. Mahon acted upon Mr. Cameron's advice and on February 18, 1914, entered into an agreement with Ledingham &
Cooper, contractors, under the direction of Cleveland and
Cameron, to reconstruct the suspension bridge. Two great
mounds of earth and rock covered the old and new anchors and
provided the setting for an attractive rock garden through which

visitors would stroll as they stepped along the platform leading to the bridge.

Gundrid Dempster: *Visitors came from far and near to see the canyon, the suspension bridge. People would come because the bridge was an outstandingly marvelous bridge! At no time were tourists allowed to run on the bridge, or was it allowed to be over-crowded. There were periodic checkups by an engineer, Mr. Cameron, to see that all was as it should be.*

Courtesy G. Dempster   *Workmen during 1914 re-construction*

Mrs. Rebbeck lived alone in the cliff house after Lilette's marriage to Edward Mahon. The Japanese workers lived in the bunkhouse; two Chinese brothers, the Mr. Lees, had built a house close by and there were two or three other residences on Capilano Road between the first canyon and the streetcar terminus. Gundrid and Waller remained in boarding school until 1915, coming home only for holidays. Winters were lonely for Mrs. Rebbeck in her isolated home, but visitors dispelled the loneliness during the season, which was mid-March to the end of September in those days.

The Capilano suspension bridge was the first commercial

Courtesy G. Dempster

Earth and rock mounds covering the cable anchors provide a peaceful garden setting.

tourist attraction in North Vancouver. It is not known exactly when collection of a fee for crossing the bridge was started but it may have been as early as 1907 when Mr. & Mrs. Copeland, who lived in a cabin north of the bridge property, were caretakers for Otto Semisch. A toll of ten cents was definitely being collected in 1911.

Gundrid Dempster: *You paid ten cents entrance fee to get into the grounds and go across the bridge and in the beginning mother would employ a man, a gatekeeper, to do that. And the gatekeeper had to be a gentleman. Not just a rough type of man.*

She usually had about three girls, girls who would come in the summer to look after the tea and so forth. The waitresses were young ladies and they slept in the teahouse, of

CAPILANO
SUSPENSION BRIDGE
ADMIT ONE

Date OCT 1 9

68

course. On the holidays she sometimes had gentlewomen to be waitresses. She had to have a certain type of woman for her teahouse, and that was known, too! I did sometimes help in the teahouse but I wasn't supposed to.

Courtesy G. Dempster

Elizabeth and Gundrid Rebbeck, Bryan Dog

We lived there through the winters, too. Just the odd person came and paid their ten cents. Mother would have had to make enough during the summer to live during the winter. When snow fell it was a lovely sight but made extra work as the snow had to be shovelled off the bridge and our cliff house roof. Once we got snowed in. The water jacket in the kitchen froze. So, we opened up the big fireplace and cooked there. We made bread. Baked it in buckets in the two fireplaces.

Courtesy G. Dempster   *The bridge in winter, c.1921*

Gundrid Dempster: *Mother kept goats. That was only tempo-*
rary. We needed milk and the goats would eat
anything. We wouldn't have to worry about
whether we had the right stuff to feed them or
not. They just ate everything — the spirea,
anything! We had Leghorn chickens. Of
course, they'd get eaten by the foxes.

The First World War changed the lives of everyone, including
the Mahons, Mrs. Rebbeck and their business at the bridge.
Rationing meant that the menu at the teahouse had to be drastically

altered to accommodate the lack of sugar, butter, flour and other staples. Prices rose on all merchandise and kept rising; and fewer visitors ventured up the Capilano Road. Government enacted legislation empowering the Canada Food Board to set regulations regarding serving and preparation of food and all public eating places were required to be licensed. Mrs. Rebbeck received a license to operate her teahouse in June 1918. In a letter to Mr. G.C. Howell of the Canada Food Board she states:

> ...*The Tea House was not operated in 1917 except for two or three days. The tea room serves light refreshments, tea, toast, sandwiches, ice cream, cake, etc. and is a great convenience to the travelling public...*

By 1921 business at the suspension bridge had improved and life was a little easier for everyone, but it would never be the same as it was before the war. Too much had changed. The bridge property was changing, too. In July 1921 Waller Rebbeck wrote to his sister Gundrid, who was now working at Calydor Sanitorium in Ontario:

Courtesy G. Dempster

Mrs. Rebbeck and her goats, Maurice and Barletta. c.1924

...We have made some improvements up here in the form of a new gate house and store combined. We sell soft drinks and ice cream, candy, tobacco, etc. in it in addition to what is sold over the counter at the tea house. At present I am storekeeper...

Courtesy G. Dempster   *The new gatehouse, 1921*

Another significant change took place at this time. Mac MacEachran arrived at Capilano sometime between 1919 and 1921 and would prove to be an important character in the continuing existence of the Capilano suspension bridge for the next 25 years.

Gundrid Dempster: *Lilette married Edward Mahon and that's really how things got started because it was his money that had the canyon. And mother fell in love with a fire warden and eventually married him. He was the fire warden on the road right up to the second canyon, looking after the fire business. That was Mac MacEachran.*

5

Years of Change

A rchibald Dunerik "Mac" MacEachran came to the Capilano area after the First World War. He was a Captain in the Royal Flying Corps, based in Egypt where he flew observation airplanes for the Army. Mac was a hard working, romantic Scotsman with a broad brogue and he worked as a ranger in the Capilano Valley.

Courtesy G. Dempster   *Mac MacEachran, c.1925*

Bryan Mahon: *Mac was the forest ranger in the Capilano Valley. He would be going up and down the valley looking for forest fires and kind of supervising, you know, the forest ranger's job. He would stop at the canyon for tea and thereby got to know Grandma. Then they got married.*

Mac MacEachran and Elizabeth Rebbeck were secretly married in August 1921. On September 17 Lilette Mahon wrote her sister Gundrid about the marriage.

> *...At present in the companionship of Mac and of the happiness of jaunting off with him on their days off and having someone with her at the Canyon, she looks fifteen years younger and very well. ...Mother has been remaking her own life quite cheerfully. ...Mac is only 26 or 27 at the most, very nice, most unselfish and kind. Bryan adores him, Edward, Waller and I like him very much...*

Courtesy G. Dempster   *Elizabeth & Mac MacEachran on front porch of the gatehouse, c.1922*

Mr. MacEachran was younger than Elizabeth by about 20 years, and his energy was much needed at the bridge. Economic conditions during the war had forced Edward Mahon and Elizabeth into a very restricted cash flow position, which meant that only essential necessities were attended to while less important matters were set aside. As a result the buildings and grounds were in need of repair and maintenance, not to mention the bridge itself. Mac had the strength and energy to tend to these matters, but where was the money going to come from?

Mac's vigor and efforts were a great addition to the management of the bridge. He advertised and popularized it and initiated additional attractions. The gate house was expanded into a pergola with a covered porch and sitting area so that passersby on the Capilano Road could refresh themselves with an ice cream or tea without having to enter the bridge grounds; and a gas station was added. Light meals were served from the pergola and the tea house was used only on holidays.

Mac MacEachran was an influential co-manager of the property. He knew that expectations of tourists had changed since the war and people were demanding more variety for their dollars

Courtesy G. Dempster   *Gas station from inside gate, c.1920*

Vancouver Public Library

Capilano Road, pergola and entrance to grounds. c.1922

spent on leisure activities. He also realized the potential impact the Indian people could have in bringing more business to the suspension bridge. With this in mind he approached Chief Mathias Joe, son of Mary Capilano and Chief Joe Capilano, with the proposition of placing totem poles on the grounds and having other Indian art work and crafts available as souvenirs. Chief Mathias agreed with MacEachran's proposal and soon after brought two of his own poles from the Capilano Reserve (Homulcheson) and raised them on the grounds close to the bridge. This represented a complete change in direction from Elizabeth MacEachran's ideal of a genteel tea house and picnic grounds.

Stan Joseph: *I used to watch my great grand uncle carve. He had quite an influence on me. Watching him through my life, when I was young, I was only about 6 or 7, I started getting interested in Indian art. He knew I was from a chief family so he introduced me to art, like carving. Now I'm restoring all the Chief's poles. The totem poles that were done by my grand uncle who was Chief Mathias.*

Time proved that Mac MacEachran was correct in his assumption that tourists would enjoy the Indian theme at the bridge. This soon became a popular attraction that beckoned to excursionists, second only to the thrill of crossing the bridge.

The novelty was overshadowed, however, by a down-turn in the economy. The Great Depression laid its heavy hand on the world and squeezed. Once again people were struggling to survive and trips to the first Capilano canyon in North Vancouver

Courtesy N. Stibbard   *Chief Mathias Joe Capilano in ceremonial garments.*

First totem poles on suspension bridge site. Carved by Chief Mathias Joe Capilano.

L. Raskewicz

became listed under "Frivolous Pastimes". The MacEachrans did their best to encourage travellers to visit their unique surroundings and it was during this time that Mac christened the bridge "The Eighth Wonder of the World". No amount of advertising and promotion could entice more visitors, however, and the MacEachrans and Mahons struggled along with everyone else. From 1927 to 1933 the gross income at the bridge averaged $5,500. a year; operating expenses were $4,900., leaving a net income of only $600. By June 31, 1935, gross receipts had decreased almost 50% and the net income dwindled to a mere $350.

The depression brought Aage Madsen and Karl Hansen to the canyon looking for work, food and lodging. Mr. & Mrs. MacEachran invited them into their home for a meal and during conversation learned that both men were experienced carvers. Not a person to let any opportunity slip by, MacEachran offered the men room and board in return for some carvings. They agreed. Madsen and Hansen stayed at the canyon long enough to produce many of the outstanding carvings that stand on the grounds today.

Stan Joseph: *Aage Madsen did a really good job on those statues. Especially the famous one of the lady with her hands up in the air. That's one that I just finished restoring. I guess it's famous because it's partly naked and it depicts the way an Indian woman actually looks.*

The two men were content with the arrangement with the MacEachrans but left the canyon when better times offered them another chance to pursue their ambitions. Aage Madsen returned to the bridge many years later and was again employed to carve statues, but in a much different way.

The season at the bridge was April–September between 1921 and 1935. It was difficult for people to get to the canyon in winter, so there was no point in keeping the tea house and bridge open at that time of year. This put an enormous strain on a very tight

Aage Madsen carved this statue during the Great Depression.

L. Raskewicz

Another statue by Madsen depicts Mrs. Mary Capilano carrying her son, Mathias Joe, on her back.

L. Raskewicz

budget.

Mr. MacEachran had friends who ran an import/export business and owned a warehouse in Papeete, Tahiti. They needed people to work for them at varying times during the year and engaged MacEachran to alternate running the warehouse and working on their ships from November to February. This commitment lasted two or three winters.

Bryan Mahon: *Now, it was in the Great Depression and they didn't make any money out of the bridge at ten cents a head, and 100 or 200 people on a weekend, and for half the year there was just no revenue. So, in the winter Mac went down to Tahiti because the bridge didn't make enough money. Grandma stayed at the canyon.*

1934 was a turning point in the lives of the MacEachrans. Early that year Mac announced to Elizabeth that he had a daughter, Irene, in Scotland whom he wanted to bring to the canyon. In March Elizabeth relinquished her position as official manager of the suspension bridge and tea house and Edward Mahon contracted MacEachran to run the business. Elizabeth wrote to her daughter —

...Edward signed an agreement with Mac by which Mac becomes the lessee of the Canyon and will run the place. Mac & Irene came to the Canyon last Thursday. So we are all three settling down to the new life and I hope it will be a happy one...

In September MacEachran started building a house on a piece of property he had acquired across the road from the bridge.

September 31 ...Mac is busy building a house on the other side of the road. You will remember where the little tea place of those other people was. The house will have 3 bedrooms, a sitting room, a kitchen with a "dinette" and a basement with furnace and garage. The old house here, with all its joys and sorrows, will become part of past history...

October 7...The house on the other side of the road is growing up and will be shingled next week ...It will have...siding and stucco on the outside and a roof of hand-split shingles tinted green. I think it will be very nice. I love this old shack but you don't put new wine into old bottles, and this old shack needs repairs.

By the end of October the MacEachran family — Mac, Elizabeth and Mac's daughter Irene — had moved out of the cliff house and into their new home.

Elizabeth Rebbeck MacEachran died February 12, 1935, after a short illness. In March Edward Mahon cancelled the insurance on the cliff house and had it torn down along with the bunkhouse. In July he sold the canyon property to Mac MacEachran. The Mackay and Mahon eras had come to an end together.

Mr. MacEachran remained at the canyon another ten years. Business improved during that time, but facilities at the bridge didn't change. For a short period he employed a three-piece orchestra to play background music while visitors enjoyed their tea in the tea house, served by young women in crisp black dresses with starched white headbands pinned neatly to their tidy hair in the finest European tradition. This may have been what attracted the next investor to the bridge, who was French.

6

Dormant Interval

Louis Henri Isadore Aubeneau sailed into Vancouver in 1908 on a French Navy vessel. As the ship slowly moved up Burrard Inlet he was struck by the beauty of the north shore, particularly that area which he would later know as Sentinel Hill on Baby Mountain in West Vancouver. He vowed he would own that hill one day and eventually he did purchase a large part of the area.

Henri Aubeneau enjoyed the amenities of early Vancouver and responded to its youthful enthusiasm for adventuresome entrepreneurs. He left the French Navy and launched a new career as a restauranteur, starting first as a waiter, then advancing to maitre d' and manager, finally opening his own establishment, Le Restaurant Francais, on Pender Street about 1938. He was associated with the well-known London Grill on Granville Street and the Hotel de France.

Mr. Aubeneau started acquiring property on Sentinel Hill very early, buying whenever property and finances became available. He was twice forced to sell his holdings due to depressions but by 1938 had accummulated 27 acres of prime development property on the hill. In June 1938 the Vancouver Sun reported —

One of the most important realty transactions of recent years in West Vancouver is reported by L.D. Orr, agent for the vendor, Henri Aubeneau. The property concerned is a site of approximately six acres known as Sentinel Crest...Clearing and grading of streets, installation of water service, etc., and subdivision of the property into some eighty homesites has just been completed ...and...is evidence that the confidence Mr. Aubeneau has maintained in the future of the property and of West Vancouver has been amply justified.

He later sold another tract to A.J.T. Taylor, as reported in this item from The Province October 8, 1938:

Sale of a tract of six acres of north shore property known as Sentinel Hill, opposite Prospect Point, is announced by H.A. Roberts Ltd. Purchaser was A.J.T. Taylor, formerly associated with British Pacific Properties Ltd., now visiting in England. Vendor is Henri Aubeneau...The property is unsuitable for subdivision but it is stated that the site would make a magnificent estate or resort hotel.

In 1945 Mr. Aubeneau offered to purchase the "Eighth Wonder of the World" from Mac MacEachran. His offer was accepted. Aubeneau, then about 62 years old, had been buying property on the north shore since he arrived in Canada in 1908; the bridge and adjoining property were added to his list of acquisitions. The package included MacEachran's home across the road from the bridge, which Henri and his wife Younette occupied soon after the purchase. The Vancouver Sun reported the sale this way on October 29, 1945:

The privately-owned suspension bridge, one of Vancouver's best known tourist attractions, was sold today for $120,000. The new owner, Henri Aubeneau, 2256 Franklin, today assured

The Vancouer Sun that the structure, with sur-
rounding improvements, would go on being a
major tourist drawing card, with no increased toll
to the public. The bridge, one of the most famous
cable pedestrian structures in the world, was sold
by A.D. McEachran, 3650 Capilano, North Van-
couver. Mr. Aubeneau also owns approximately
30 acres of property adjoining the bridge. This
will be cleared and improved chiefly for the benefit
of youngsters....

The Aubeneaus didn't make any improvements to the property or expand the business in any way. In fact, they ignored the
potential for expansion and seemed content to collect the entrance
fee and sell a few hotdogs from the concession at the gate. The
beautiful teahouse, which once received the Duchess of Connaught and Princess Patricia, was ignored and misused as a
storeroom for odds and ends. In addition, the beautiful carvings
of Aage Madsen and Karl Hansen were covered with tar, suppos-
edly to preserve them.

Henri and Younette Aubeneau operated the business in their
unique way for 8 years.

Rae Mitchell: *The Aubeneaus had no children. After the*
                       first Mrs. Aubeneau died, Henry married
                       another lady who lived up the (Fraser) valley
                       someplace. She came to live with Henry for a
                       while but it didn't stick. So Henry was on his
                       own again. He died shortly after that. Henry
                       had never been back to France. He left (his
                       estate) to a nephew in France whom he had
                       never seen.

Henri Aubeneau died in December 1960. Vancouver oldtim-
ers will remember his popular London Grill and Le Restaurant
Francais cafes. Not many will recall that he once owned the
Capilano suspension bridge.

7

Shaking off
the Dust

W hen Douglas McRae "Rae" Mitchell was about 17 years
old he went to work for his father and uncle in the heating and
plumbing business for $5.00 a week. In 1933, when Rae was 23
and the Great Depression was well under way, he bought his
uncle's share of the firm and became a full partner in Mitchell
Bros. Rae and his father worked hard and over the years created
a very successful business. When Rae's father was ready to retire
he sold his interest in the company to his son, who continued to
provide service to households in Vancouver until he retired in
1951.

Rae Mitchell became interested in the Capilano suspension
bridge in 1948, when he and his family moved from Vancouver to
a home on Capilano Road, about a mile north of the bridge. The
business had become dormant under Henri Aubeneau's management and Rae was enticed by the potential he could see for the
bridge to become a very worthwhile economic venture.

Rae Mitchell: *Several times I asked Henri if he would like
to sell the bridge because he wasn't doing a
great deal with it. Actually, they weren't
doing very much business.*

At the end of March 1953, Henri phoned me at home and asked me to come down to see him. His wife had died about a month before. So, I went down and he asked me if I still wanted to buy the bridge. We talked about it and he set a price and before I went home I bought it. All my friends kind of laughed at me, thinking "Why didn't you buy the Brooklyn Bridge", or something. They thought I was a little bit crazy, I think.

Courtesy N. Stibbard

Entrance to Capilano Suspension Bridge, c.1955

Mitchell was still a young man with lots of energy to meet new challenges. He went to work. The buildings were cleaned up, gardens were reclaimed and improved and the bridge started to laugh again.

Rae Mitchell: *Henri was rather careful. When I bought (the bridge) there was an old building at the entrance where the present gate is now. In the south end of that they had an old oil stove and made hot dogs, with hot water to cook them in. I well remember when we were taking stock*

87

*with old Henri, the big pot on the stove. So, old
Henri and I were going around marking things
down and he takes the lid off this pot. He had
a fork and he started to go around in this
greasy water that had been there since September and he says "Two weiners.". And I
marked them down. ...*

*The main building hadn't been used for
years, not since MacEachran. It was full of old
paint cans, ...cans with old bent nails and all
kinds of junk. Henry listed it all. I got some of
the fellows who worked for the District to work
at night and Saturdays and Sundays to help me
clean it out. It took about a month.*

*Henri never threw anything away, he sold
it to me! That's what I meant when I said he
was careful.*

The first thing Mitchell did was re-open the tea house, but with
significant changes. A new wing was added to the east side and
incorporated into the original building to form a banquet room
called the Thunderbird Room.

His first major improvement was greeted by opposition from
his neighbours and certain special interest groups, but Rae
Mitchell's years as a successful businessman in Vancouver had
taught him to be thorough.

Rae Mitchell: *We started building in 1953, as soon as I
bought the bridge. When I bought the bridge
North Vancouver was in receivership. They'd
gone bankrupt. Sam Sowden was the commis-
sioner in charge. I enquired through him
about the bridge and he said "Rae, you can do
anything with it as long as it's an improvement.". So, I told him what I had in mind and
he said that was fine, come and get a permit. I*

got Charlie VanNorman, the architect, to draw up a plan for that room. I got a permit. The building inspector then was Vic Lonsdale, an old North Vancouver resident. That permit became quite valuable later on because as soon as we started building we had everybody in North Vancouver objecting, including the Women's Temperance League.

Unfortunately, the head of the league for the lower mainland lived in North Vancouver. Well, you'd think that I was the worst! We weren't going to get a liquor license anyway. Never thought of it, because you couldn't get them in banquet rooms. The people who had the banquet had to get the permit. But if I hadn't got that building permit from Sam Sowden I would have been in trouble with all this.

The Thunderbird Room opened in November 1953, with Margaret Watson as its first hostess. It became a very popular location for wedding receptions and other special banquets. A promotional advertisement stated the Thunderbird Room was a short 15-minute drive from downtown Vancouver. (This would have been via the Lions Gate Bridge, which was foreseen by George Mackay in 1890.) It was a mere twinkling compared to the length of time it took a visitor from Vancouver to reach the bridge in 1911, the year the original tea house was built.

The controversy persisted, however, and on May 11, 1954, the Vancouver Province ran this item:

Residents Protest 'Dine-Dance' Noise — North Van District Council Plans Probe...The complaint was made by R.E. Homewood...spokesman for residents near Canyon Gardens and Capilano Scenic Attractions at the suspension *bridge...Squabble between residents and the two establishments came to a head when the latter made formal application to council for cabaret licences. 'That was 13 weeks ago,' said Homewood, 'and nothing has been done yet...The noise and drinking is going on the same as before.'. Reeve C.E. Scanlan replied, 'The matter has more or less died a natural death. We have heard nothing from the applicants. Apparently they don't want licences.' 'I'm aware of that,' said Homewood. 'They are content with the present $2. liquor permit setup.' On motion of Councillor George Sargeant, council agreed to conduct a 'full investigation' to determine if the establishments are operating contrary to district by-laws.*

Rae Mitchell's Thunderbird Room continued to operate for the next seven years.

Rae Mitchell: *It was very profitable and we were busy all the time. In fact, towards the end we would close it down about the end of May and clear out all the tables and turn it into a gift shop. When we closed at the end of May we had a lot of people putting pressure on us for wedding receptions in June. It got so that they were almost in tears when they couldn't have their reception here. Eventually we closed it right off. While it was profitable, it meant that we had to have staff on until 1:00 or 2:00 in the morning and at any banquet there is generally one person who causes trouble. Anytime you have alcohol somebody gets too much and... As the tourist business increased we decided it would be less bother and just as profitable to have it as a gift shop all the time.*

Another controversy arose when Mr. Mitchell started advertising the "World Famous Suspension Bridge" on Mayne Island in the Strait of Georgia. W.A.C. Bennett was the Premier of British Columbia then, and Phil Gaglardi was his Highways Minister. It all started in June 1963.

Rae Mitchell: *We had five signs down in the state of Washington, on the highway north of Oregon. The traffic was increasing going over to Vancouver Island, particularly to Victoria, so I found a nice grassy point on Mayne Island and after making quite a few inquiries discovered it belonged to the Indians. Anyway, I ended up leasing that point for five years to put a sign up. Then we prefabbed everything in Vancouver and had it all painted in panels. It was a 12x30-foot sign. Jimmy Minamimaye and Joe Negata went over there and they camped out and put it up. And that was the beginning of a controversy.*

Courtesy N. Stibbard   *Controversial Mayne Island sign, c.1963*

91

I think the first thing was in the Victoria Daily Times. They had a big cartoon. The point was covered with all kinds of signs and it created a lot more fuss ...

Eventually it got down to the government. At that time the provincial government and the Tourist Bureau of Victoria had signs down in Washington. Their sign was "Follow the Birds to Victoria". The provincial government thought I should take this sign of ours down. Well, it was getting us a lot of free publicity. It was written up here and a lot of

"Look! Quick! That's Mayne Island...right between Dr. Skull's Cornplasters and Filter Flip Cigarettes!"

other places in the newspapers and whatnot. Best sign in the world, I thought.

So, I wrote them and I said you've got so many signs in the State of Washington; maybe the people there don't like your signs. When you take those down I'll consider taking mine down. Then they said they were going to try and force me to take it down. I said if you become any more of a nuisance to me I'm going to put in a lighting plant and light the sign at night. Then it kind of died down.

Another area that received Mr. Mitchell's early attention was the garden, which had been allowed to return to a wild state and was overgrown with blackberry vines and huckleberries.

Rae Mitchell: *The garden was a mess. I got a Japanese gardener in there, with about 6 or 7 men, and they worked for a long time. Then I hired one of them. I watched him and I said, that's the fellow I want to work for me, and he worked ever since. His name was Jimmy Minamimaye. He worked for me from 1953 until this year (1987) — 34 years.*

His brother-in-law, Joe Negata, he worked for us I guess 30 years. But Jimmy was the boss. And he would still be working except he got cancer. It's one of those things that shouldn't happen — not to someone who's never been sick. He was the healthiest guy in the world. That's the way it goes. We miss him very much.

Courtesy Mrs. J. Minamimaye   *Jimmy Minamimaye, head gardener.*

I developed the other side (of the canyon). In 1955 or '56 we got in some equipment and we made three ponds...We brought the machinery in from the West Vancouver side and scooped out those ponds. Then we diverted a small creek that ran through there so it runs through the ponds and then out so it makes a little waterfall where the tourists can see it. We keep fish in the ponds. The kids in the British Properties come over and catch the fish. So, we have to get new fish every year. It's like stealing apples. It gets them up early, anyway!

L. Raskewicz

L. Raskewicz

1956 was the year of a major facelift for the bridge. In 1914 Edward Mahon added a second cable to the one installed by William Farrell in 1903. These two original cables would now be replaced by the first pre-stressed cable made in British Columbia.

Rae Mitchell: *We actually didn't know when I bought the bridge there were two cables...of different construction, different diameters. We didn't have any way that we could tell what their condition was and they'd been there since 1914. So, rather than take a chance on them I decided I'd rebuild the complete bridge. We built a whole new bridge. New crosspieces, the decking.*

First of all, I went to one of the ship building companies, one of the local ones here, to get a quotation from them. They wanted thirty days to build the bridge, to re-place it. Add that to the cost of building the bridge, what we'd lose in revenue, it would be pretty steep. Then I went on my own and got Bob McLellan and as soon as we decided how we would do it I got everything prefabricated.

Just about that time British Wire Ropes had put in a pre-stressing machine so these were the first pre-stressed cables made in British Columbia. That is, they put a tension on the cable after it's made, by the pre-stressing machine. These cables are pre-stressed to 100,000 pounds each. So they put on an excess of that to make sure that the cable has that capacity. Everything on the bridge comes under that category of 100,000 pounds.

Instead of putting two cables in, I had a shackle designed by Bob McLellan, who is a wire rope engineer. We had one cable and a large forged shackle and two 45-foot cables on either side and at both ends that go back to the anchor. The place that the wear comes on the bridge is where the cable goes over the roller as soon as it gets to the land. The cable goes back and forth there. If there is any wear we can take out one 45-foot section and the other one would hold the bridge. Then we could replace it and do that at both ends of the bridge. Every year we have the bridge inspected by a professional wire rope engineer, both for our own satisfaction and for our liability insurance. To date, with this new modern cable, there is absolutely no sign of wear because it's more flexible. The older cable was not as flexible.

Bob McLellan did most of the engineering for the new bridge because he was a wire rope engineer. But the ideas were mine. I built it

North Shore Museum & Archives

Reeve Grant Currie on new bridge, 1957

*from Monday morning at 8:00 to 4:30 on
Friday afternoon, instead of thirty days. And
I used Commonwealth Construction to put the
cables in. They put the cables in in one day and
took the other ones out. They had a big truck
with a winch out on the road and we built a
trestle across the garden so that when the new
cable was drawn out it was being hauled out by
the old cable coming back and they just
winched it up onto the truck.*

*British Wire Rope were interested in the
old cable to see what it would stand. So they
put it on the pre-stressing machine and it
wouldn't break at 100,000 pounds! But it gave
us peace of mind anyway.*

About this time Rae Mitchell became acquainted with Aage
Madsen. Madsen had come up to the bridge for a visit and was
astonished to see his carvings covered with black tar. Mr. Mitchell
asked his advice about the best way to remove the tar and restore
the statues to their original state. It seemed that the only way to
restore them was to have the tar carved off, so Mitchell hired
Madsen to do the job. When he was finished the carvings looked
like they had when he created them 20 years earlier.

When Elizabeth and Mac MacEachran moved from the cliff
house to their new home across the road in 1935, it marked the end
of a twenty-five year period of continuous residence at the bridge
site. Employees would occasionally be housed in two bedrooms
upstairs in the tea house, but this was seasonal. Rae Mitchell
provided an opportunity for the tea house to be occupied again, on
a permanent basis, when he met Walter Taylor.

Walter was introduced to Mr. Mitchell through Reg Deakin,
who was a good friend of Mitchell's. Rae was approached on the
possibility that he might have a job for Walter, who was deaf,
and who had skills Mitchell knew could be useful at the bridge. He
gave Walter a job and also a place to live.

Rae Mitchell: *At that time we had the banquets so Walter lived in one of the rooms upstairs and he did his cooking in the kitchen down below. We gave him things to do and, in fact, he was at the gate a lot of the time because it was a job that he could do. He could read your lips...he could talk as well. He was bright. He was a great photographer, too. That was his hobby. We kept him because he was honest and he filled a niche. Everybody liked him. I think Walter must have been here maybe close to fifteen years, something like that. We didn't keep any record. He had to retire a number of years ago and we kept him on a small pension; and he got his old age pension and a company pension, so he did alright. Walter was maybe a year older than I am. He died last year. We were very fond of him.*

Walter Taylor was living at the bridge in October 1962 when the remnants of Hurricane Freda blew over the greater Vancouver area.

Rae Mitchell: *It was kind of a spot hurricane. I guess most hurricanes hit here and then they move and then they hit somewhere else. That particular one did a lot of damage in Stanley Park and then it came over and picked on us.*

We had two big trees, which I can show you the stumps of, they came right through the building. Walter, I guess he felt the vibrations when the trees hit. They almost hit him; came right above him. He phoned me up and he says "Mr. Mitchell, I heard a funny noise here. I think you'd better come down." That was the understatement of the year! By that time it was pouring rain. The showcases were broken and all the floors were flooded. I had to drill holes in the floor to let the water out. We had a lot of glass showcases where we kept the jewelry and other things; they were all smashed. It was a mess.

The big totem poles out by the canyon, they were down. We had eight trees down on the bridge. All together we had eighty-two big trees down. It was a mess. The ones laying on the bridge, of course, we had to get experts in to cut them off. I had a fellow by the name of Vince Bonner come in to cut them up into lengths so we could get them hauled out. Vince was an old friend of mine. He was cutting one on the far side and it sprang up when it released and it threw him right out into the canyon. He ended up way down at the bottom of the canyon and was in the hospital for about five or six weeks. It's a wonder it didn't kill him. It would've except that he was a pretty strong person.

Elizabeth MacEachran had her animal companions — cats, dogs, chickens, goats, and the occasional skunk. Mr. Mitchell had his donkeys.

Rae Mitchell: *It was at the time of the earthquake up in Alaska. The aftermath of that was that they had a flood. A tidal wave came up the Alberni Canal and flooded part of Port Alberni — the lower part. One of the clubs, the Lions or one of those clubs, had this big auction at the Agrodome (to help the people who had been flooded out). We went there and I think I bought some garden furniture. People weren't bidding, so when these two donkeys came up I thought, well, everything's too cheap, I'll help them a bit and I'll bid them up. I was bidding them up and all of a sudden the auctioneer says "The two donkeys belong to that man over there!", and he was pointing right at me. So there we were. I had to pay for them.*

But actually, I didn't mind getting them but then the problem was to get them to the suspension bridge. I phoned up an old friend of mine...who had a horse trailer and he said he'd come out and get them. Well, maybe you can get horses in a horse trailer but donkeys are a different story! It took all day to get these donkeys in but eventually we made it.

Then after we got them they wouldn't eat. We couldn't find out what they'd been fed on before so eventually we tried out all the different kinds of hay. They'd eat oats but we had to get them to eat hay. They would eat only the most expensive alfalfa hay, which we fed them for years and years, until one of them developed a bad foot and the vet couldn't fix it. And the last one — one of our summer employees, her parents ran a farm in Kelowna so they came and took it. They were at the bridge a long time. The last one was around until two years ago (1986). They must have been awfully old.

Many employees came and went over the years. A good number of them were university students who worked successive summers making money for their next year's school expenses. Some were permanent employees, like Donna Hilton, who was Mitchell's secretary at the time of the bear.

Rae Mitchell:

A number of years ago I had a young girl who worked here since she got out of high school, Donna Hilton. She was kind of my Girl Friday. She did everything and ran the shop. Did a very good job of it, too. I had gone home on this particular Sunday. It was in August, I believe.

I had gone home for supper and she called me and she said "There's a man here who says there's a bear across the river." Well, we got bears — I got them up at my house quite often — but being that this is fenced I was a little surprised. So, I said "I'll come down and in the meantime you phone the RCMP and they'll get the predatory hunter."

It only took me about five minutes to get down here and by that time the bear had come down the canyon, up this side and he was right by the end of the bridge. Just about that time, maybe five minutes later, the predatory hunter came with two dogs. The dogs got the smell of the bear and away they went down the canyon. The hunter couldn't follow them because it's almost vertical. About two days later the predatory hunter came in and wanted to know if we'd seen one of his dogs. We said we hadn't and he said "Well, I haven't seen it since either." We never did hear what happened to it.

But the funny part of the story was that it was an American who told Donna that there was a bear across the river. He said "I've just been up in Alaska and I spent eight or nine thousand dollars to try and hunt a bear, and this is the first one I've seen!"

Rae Mitchell continued to improve and expand the Capilano suspension bridge holdings. When the opportunity arose he purchased the MacEachran/Aubeneau home and an adjacent residence which was also a gift shop. These two properties are now the Bridge House Restaurant and the Canyon House Galleria.

Gordon Prentice purchased the Aubeneau home from Henri's estate in 1961. He made some minor renovations and leased the building to Mr. Wann, who operated a restaurant there. Later it was run by Dave McNicholl and Paul Berrittoni. The restaurant was known as the Chelsea House for some time, and as the Hobbit House until January 1988.

Rae Mitchell: *When I bought it from Gordon Prentice Mr. Wann was operating it as a restaurant. So he continued on. Mrs. Wann worked there and I think they had only one or two waitresses. Then Mrs. Wann became very ill and he couldn't handle it by himself. He had a very nice business and he was a pretty good person. He wanted to sell it and he sold to Ray Marinakus at the Canyon Gardens, who ran it until the end of Mr. Wann's lease. At that time two boys — Dave McNicholl and Paul Berrittoni — they leased it for about ten years. Their lease ran out this month (January 1988) so we terminted their lease and Nancy intends to run it herself, with a manager.*

Gordon and Lucy Prentice also owned the Canyon House, where they lived and operated a small china and gift shop. Mitchell acquired this property and increased the variety of items available there.

Rae Mitchell: *We developed other retail stores and started up a wholesale business. Actually, it*

*was on account of our volume of business at
the suspension bridge; it got so that we were
buying direct from the manufacturers, princi-
pally in the Orient. To get rid of the volume
that we had to buy in we went selling it to other
people. Now our wholesale business extends
from coast to coast. We have a warehouse in
North Vancouver and a similar one in Mark-
ham, Ontario. We have an office and show-
room in Montreal and (Oceanic Cost Plus)
retail stores in Coquitlam, Gastown, Victoria
and Canada Place. The business has grown a
bit.*

After 18 years Rae Mitchell managed to shake the dust off the
suspension bridge and turn it into gold. His energy, astute
business sense and nerve had enabled him to develop the Capilano
suspension bridge into a significant element of the British Columbia tourist industry. In 1971 he decided it was time to start
preparing for his second retirement, so he approached his two
daughters and their husbands, Gail and Bob McFarland, and
Nancy and John Stibbard, with a proposal that he felt would
benefit them all.

Rae Mitchell: *That would have been when I gave them a
management contract so that they could make
some money out of it, and a profit. I sold them
just the stock in trade and let them operate (the
business). Then later on I sold them the
property, that is the real estate. That was in
1976.*

Mr. Mitchell still has his office at the bridge and is there for
part of nearly every day. He has left his mark beside those of
George Grant Mackay, Bruno Stelzer, Edward Mahon, Mac
MacEachran and Henri Aubeneau. His daughter Nancy is next.

Courtesy R. Mitchell   *Rae Mitchell*

8

Into the Future

Nancy Rae Mitchell Stibbard was about eight years old when her father put her to work serving ice cream in the concession at the gatehouse. Everybody used to ask for her, or point to "that girl", because she made such great big ice cream cones for ten cents.

Courtesy N. Stibbard

Nancy Stibbard:

From that point on I worked in the store here almost every summer. I remember working for thirty-five cents an hour, until my father could no longer get away with that! I think he finally raised it to eighty-five cents.

Nancy and Rae Mitchell, c.1956

Nancy Stibbard and two members of the British track team who competed in the 1954 British Empire & Commonwealth Games in Vancouver.

All the athletes came here. I remember having my picture taken with every great big handsome fellow that came in the door. I was still in pigtails at that time.

Through the years we've always had a number of celebrities that have come in. As a youngster I found that quite exciting. We've had Anthony Quinn; I think we had some rather notorious playboy centerfolds. I can remember a movie that was done here with a well-known movie star. She was a sex kitten type and she was being chased across the bridge. My father would remember better as he has a good memory for that kind of event. We've had Bob Hope here, as well as a number of famous pop stars.

Courtesy N. Stibbard　　　　　*Gail Mitchell with Amos & Andy, c.1956*

When Nancy was growing up she never thought about owning the bridge. She was too busy enjoying her own life and setting different patterns. Her mother advised her to stay out of business and pursue a career in nursing, or teaching, or some other profession. A business career was far down the road when Nancy received her Masters degree in psychology from the University of British Columbia in 1968. Nancy recalls how she reacted when her father approached her and her sister Gail about running the business.

Nancy Stibbard:　　　*I had never really thought about that. No, I had no intention of running it. My father suggested that it would be a good idea if he were to sell it to us. So, we agreed on the understanding that our husbands would actually run the business.*

My sister's husband ran (the bridge) for a few years while my husband ran the wholesale

*end. He still runs it. Eventually it was decided
that it would be better if just one side of the
family ran the business. The Stibbards took
over. At that point, again, I had no intention of
becoming totally involved in running the
company. However, as you can see, I am
running it.*

Nancy was content with what she was doing outside of the
business. She was very involved in volunteer work, played tennis,
skiied and enjoyed her roles as mother and wife. She hired a
general manager to look after the bridge.

Nancy Stibbard: *I took on (the business) about four years
ago (1983) and hired a general manager right
away, but he didn't work out. He lasted about
four months. It was so traumatic for me to let
him go that I thought, I can't go through that
again! So, I decided I'd do it and I've been
running it as the owner and operator ever
since. I had to learn a lot about business in one
really big hurry. I didn't even know how to
read a balance sheet when I started out. It's
been interesting.*

*There are two separate companies. The
wholesale is called Capilano Trading Ltd. It
actually originated out of this business because when we began here it was very difficult
to buy merchandise in Canada. We had to
import a lot of product, plus other people
wanted to buy from us, so the natural thing to
do was split it off. It has become quite a big
company.*

*But in this store (at the bridge) we do not
import very much at all. It's almost exclu-
sively Canadian. We pride ourselves in our se-*

L. Raskewicz   *The Trading Post*

lection of merchandise...and we're always looking for new and more interesting products. Things from up north in terms of handmade knitwear, handmade mucklucks with beautiful beading and fur and so on. Trying to achieve that perfect mix is a great challenge.

111

Mrs. Stibbard also runs the Canyon House Galleria, the house and business her father purchased from Gordon Prentice. The Galleria offers visitors an eclectic selection of fine china, handcrafts, art and antiques.

L. Raskewicz   *Canyon House Galleria*

Nancy Stibbard: *Originally it was a small house similar to the Bridge House. We used to sell English teacups and teapots. About three or four years before I came here my brother-in-law decided that it should be expanded and that's when we turned it into the size of the building that it is now.*

The Galleria is different. It's an import store composed of exclusive lines. Waterford, English china, leather goods, German crystal and figurines. It's very different from the Trading Post.

Nancy Stibbard finds the tourist business an interesting and exciting challenge.

Nancy Stibbard: *People within the industry are very friendly, very cooperative. There's never a feeling of competition among us. We share information and support each other's attractions, hotels, or whatever. Everybody benefits in the end from that attitude. Plus, you're not having to get out there and sell something that people don't want. You're involved with people who are on holiday and are looking for fun. Usually they're in a good frame of mind so what we have to do is provide them with hospitality and an entertaining experience.*

L. Raskewicz

An Easter bunny hiding eggs during the Easter Egg Hunt in 1988.

Nancy has a simple philosophy about how to treat visitors at the bridge.

Nancy Stibbard: *We encourage our staff to be as friendly and cooperative as they possibly can. Hospitality should be our main attraction; then the suspension bridge.*

We do a lot of staff training. We like our staff to think that everyone who walks in that gate is a guest, not a customer, and that they are to be treated as a guest would be treated in their own home. We work very hard on that philosophy.

In the summertime there are about 75 employees; in the wintertime probably about 40 some odd. As you can imagine, we keep a lot of students employed. They like it here and they come back year after year until they finish school. And they even come back and visit us long after they have gone on to other things.

L. Raskewicz   *A friendly staff member at the entrance gate.*

During the last four years Mrs. Stibbard introduced various new programs which she felt would add to the visitors' enjoyment of their bridge experience.

Nancy Stibbard: *We're trying to always add to the experience that people get when they come here. They do have to pay an admission, so we've introduced things like anthropology tours so*

L. Raskewicz   *Stan Joseph, Squamish carver.*

that the tourist can get some understanding of why Indians carve poles and what they mean; a little bit about their history; a little bit about the different tribes in this area.

We also do nature tours as we have a virgin forest on the other side of the bridge. We have students who take people around the trails and explain to them about the types of trees and their age... And we have an Indian carver on site at all times and he likes to chat with tourists as well.

Occasionally, when visiting dignitaries are expected, security at the bridge becomes a concern.

Nancy Stibbard: *Last year (1986) we had two RCMP come in to check us out for security because the Prince of Spain was coming. It was all quite exciting. I was asked to give him and his entourage a tour of our property. He was very affable.*

In January 1988 Nancy Stibbard renovated the Hobbit House and re-opened it as the Bridge House. This was the first of several improvements she has planned for the centennial celebration in 1989, commemorating construction of the first bridge.

L. Raskewicz

Bridge House Restaurant Original building built in 1935 by Mac MacEachran.

Nancy Stibbard: *I've taken over the restaurant across the street and we're going to do the best job we can. We've hired a really fine chef and an excellent manager. It will be good for the local clientele as well as the tourists that come to the bridge.*

Part of the facelifting program Nancy put together for 1988 involves giving the entire complex a unified look. She wants people to know that the Capilano suspension bridge experience is on both sides of Capilano Road and not just inside the admission gate.

L. Raskewicz

Bridge House Restaurant and Canyon House Galleria on Capilano Road

One hundred years have passed since George Mackay stood on the edge of the canyon and gazed down at the Capilano River two hundred feet below. He had a vision of the Capilano canyon as a recreational wonderland, but did not live long enough to see

118

his vision become reality. Nancy Stibbard has seen that reality, and more. Nearly two million visitors come to the bridge every year from all over the world. They enjoy the thrill of crossing the deep, rocky canyon on the gently swaying suspension bridge to experience the peacefulness of the tall cedars on the other side.

At the moment Nancy Stibbard is busy with plans for the 1989 centennial celebration. After that she'll think about the future — for she is the future — of the laughing bridge.

L. Raskewicz   *Nancy Stibbard*

L. Raskewicz

Capilano Suspension Bridge

Bibliography

Baker, Lawrence
Dempster, Gundrid
Joseph, Stan
Mahon, Bryan
Mitchell, Rae
North Shore Museum &Archives
North Vancouver, Corp. of the District of
North Vancouver Public Library
Stibbard, Nancy
University of British Columbia
Vancouver City Archives
Vancouver Land Registry Office
Vancouver Public Library

A History of the Japanese Canadians in B.C., 1958
Barr, Capt. James — *Ferry Across the Harbour*
Bourdon, Don — *Early Recreational Business in Capilano, North Vancouver, B.C., 1900–1939*, 1975
Burns, J. Rodger — *Saga of a Municipality in Its Formative Days, 1891–1907*
Canadian Encyclopedia, first edition
Khahtsahlano, August Jack and Charlie, Domanic — *Squamish Legends*
Matthews, Major J.S. — *Early Vancouver*
Mitchell, Evelyn — *Klahowya Tillicum*
Morton, James W. — *Capilano: The Story of a River*
Vancouver Automobile Club — *Footpaths Around Vancouver*, c.1915

Index

Back Cover Photo: Courtesy B. Mahon
Japanese contractors at mouth of Capilano River,
flume in background, c.1910